AF428107

HOW DID THE ANCIENT CARTHAGE RULE?

Ancient History Books for Kids Grade 4

Children's Ancient History

In this book, we're going to talk about Ancient Carthage and when its citizens ruled the Mediterranean Sea. So, let's get right to it!

WHERE WAS CARTHAGE?

If you locate the modern-day country of Tunisia on a map of the countries on the Mediterranean Sea coast, then you'll know where the ancient city of Carthage was located. At one time, during its golden age, Carthage controlled a great deal of the sea's coastline. The ruling powers there controlled North Africa, the southern part of Spain, and the islands of Sardinia as well as Sicily and Corsica.

Ancient site of Carthage

Mediterranean Sea

Just as it is today, the Mediterranean Sea was a very important waterway for transportation as well as trade. Carthage developed a powerful navy and this helped them to stay in control for a long time as the Greeks and Romans became more powerful.

HOW LONG WAS CARTHAGE A POWER BASE?

Legends about the city's history say that Carthage was founded by Queen Elissa, also called Queen Dido. She was queen of the city of Tyre in the Phoenician Empire and founded Carthage, whose name means "new city" around 814 BC. After Alexander the Great conquered the wealthy city of Tyre in 332 BC, the rich citizens from Tyre fled and came to Carthage, which helped to make the city more powerful.

Alexander the Great

Carthage

At the beginning, Carthage was only a small seaport on the coastline. Phoenician travelers would stop there to pick up supplies or to repair pieces of their ships so they could travel on the Mediterranean Sea once again. The citizens from Tyre began to establish the city as a central hub for trade. They drove the Africans who were already living there out of the area or took them as slaves.

Less than one hundred years later, Carthage had become the wealthiest city in all of the Mediterranean area. The upper class lived in elaborate *palaces* and even the middle class had attractive dwellings. Monies that came in from both tributes as well as tariffs added to the city's wealth along with the high-profit businesses specializing in international trade.

Carthage ruins

The most glorious part of the city was the harbor. There were over 220 docks. There were tall, beautiful columns and the harbor was decorated with sculptures in the Grecian style. Their trading ships sailed to ports around the Mediterranean for shipping and receiving.

The Carthaginian government built a very strong navy. It was the best in the entire area and this naval force kept them safe and provided them a way to get new territories to add to their domain.

Carthage ruins

The population of Carthage gained their independence from the Phoenician Empire in 650 BC. From then on, Carthage gained even more power and its rulers were very influential for over 500 years from 650 BC to 146 BC. During its peak, it was the most powerful of all the cities in the Mediterranean, but eventually the Roman Empire defeated Carthage in 146 BC.

THE GOVERNMENT OF CARTHAGE

At the beginning, when Carthage was part of the Phoenician Empire, it was ruled by a king. Later, its government switched to an oligarchy, which simply means that a few of the select wealthy individuals were in charge of the government. Even though the government was run by a select few, there were democratic features of their government as well.

Columns in Carthage

Punic Ruins, Carthage

They had lawmakers who were elected and there were trade unions as well as town meetings. There were judges as well and they had legal and executive powers, but no power over the military. It isn't known as to whether the judges, called suffetes, were elected by an assembly of ordinary citizens or if they were elected by an elite council of wealthy families.

There was a system of checks and balances like we have in United States democracy today. At the time the Punic Wars were started, the wealthy Barcid family was in power and they had control over the military as well as Carthage's lands outside the continent of Africa.

Carthage ruins

Island of Sicily

THE SICILIAN WARS, 580 BC to 376 BC

It wasn't easy to stay in power in the Mediterranean Sea. First Greece and then Rome were gaining in power. The island of Sicily was an important piece of land and Greece and Carthage fought over it for over 200 years.

Despite the many battles, the situation was never totally settled. For a long time, the island was split in half, with the Greeks in control of the eastern half and the Carthaginians in control of the west.

Sicily map
Tyrrhenian Sea
Aeolian Islands
Strait of Messin
Messina
Palermo
Bagheria
Peloritani Range
Nebrodi Range
Madonie Range
Mount Etna
Paterno
Acireale
Enna
Caltanissetta
Catania
Agrigento
Hyblaean Mountains
Gela
Syracuse
Vittoria
Ragusa
Modica
(km)
100
(mi)
50

Carthaginian Triremes

TREATY WITH ROME

During the time of the conflict with Greece over Sicily, in 509 BC, Carthage signed a treaty with Rome. At this point, Rome wasn't really yet a threat. Carthage had a powerful navy and Rome essentially had no navy.

Carthage was in control of the western half of the Mediterranean Sea as well as North Africa, Sardinia, and half of Sicily. They were in power so the Romans agreed to the treaty but the situation didn't last forever. The Roman Empire was growing and soon they would fight to ensure that the city of Carthage and its conquests wouldn't be a threat to Rome.

Sardinia

Carthage historic architecture

THE FIRST PUNIC WAR, 264 to 241 BC

As Rome became more powerful, its leaders decided that the expansion the Carthage Empire must be stopped. Their powerful navy had been able to keep the Romans in check up to this point, but the Romans knew that they had to gain Sicily first because the island was a "stepping stone" to all points in the Mediterranean.

At that point in time, Rome had a powerful army but no navy. However, the Romans were determined to solve that problem. They built over 300 ships. They built the ships with innovative ramps as well as gangways.

Roman Galleys

These gangways could be lowered and then secured on the surface of the enemy's ships. The reason they did this was so their soldiers could fight using the same strategies that they had used on land. Their tactics eventually worked.

After a difficult start battling the Carthaginians on both sea and land, they defeated them and took Sicily as their prize. The Romans made Carthage pay them a huge indemnity, which was basically money to make amends for the destruction they had caused Rome.

THE MERCENARY WAR, 241 to 237 BC

Soldiers who had been hired by Carthage to fight in the wars hadn't been paid so they went into battle to demand they be paid. The general Hamilcar Barca won the war against the mercenaries, but while this was happening, Rome took over the Carthaginian territories of Sardinia as well as Corsica. Carthage responded by expanding their territory in Spain.

THE SECOND PUNIC WAR, 218 to 202 BC

The famous general Hannibal, who was the son of Hamilcar Barca, invaded Italy from his position in Spain. He marched his troops over the Alps and won battle after battle on Italian soil.

Hannibal Barca

Battle of Zama

He was victorious again at the Battle of Cannae in 216 BC, but he couldn't continue to gain power because he didn't have sufficient soldiers or supplies. Fourteen years later, in 202 BC, he was defeated by Scipio Africanus, the Roman general, in Northern Africa at the Battle of Zama. Once again Rome exacted a heavy indemnity for the battle losses.

Carthage was struggling to pay off all its debts from the previous two wars with Rome. They felt that once the debt was paid, their treaty with Rome would be over, however Rome wanted them to bend to their will.

One of the prominent Roman senators ended his speeches in every case with the phrase "I believe Carthage should be burned to the ground."

THE THIRD PUNIC WAR, 149 to 146 BC

The demands escalated when Rome decided that Carthage should be taken apart and rebuilt again at a new inland location. When the government of Carthage refused, the Third Punic War began. The Romans attacked Carthage for a period of three years before the city gave up. After the Romans looted the city, they burned it completely to the ground.

Third Punic War

Carthage was a ruined city until 122 BC. Then a Roman tribune founded a colony there, but it failed, because the memories of the Punic Wars were still too fresh in people's minds.

The famous Roman leader Julius Caesar wanted to rebuild Carthage, but he was assassinated before any of those plans happened. Five years after he died, the city came back from the ashes, this time as an important colony in the Roman Empire.

Tunis Carthage ruins

The city continued to be under the influence of the Roman Empire who held it strong for centuries until 698 AD, when the Muslims destroyed the city. They founded the capital city of Tunisia, called Tunis, not too far from Carthage's ruins. Today, the ruins of the formerly powerful city of Carthage can still be seen in Tunisia.

Awesome! Now you know more about the history of Ancient Carthage. You can find more Ancient History books from Baby Professor by searching the website of your favorite book retailer.

Punic cemetery at Carthage

Visit

BABY PROFESSOR
EDUCATION KIDS

www.BabyProfessorBooks.com
to download Free Baby Professor eBooks
and view our catalog of new and exciting
Children's Books